MUSKRATS

by Meg Gaertner

Cody Koala
An Imprint of Pop!
popbooksonline.com

abdobooks.com
Published by Pop!, a division of ABDO, PO Box 398416, Minneapolis, Minnesota 55439. Copyright © 2019 by POP, LLC. International copyrights reserved in all countries. No part of this book may be reproduced in any form without written permission from the publisher. Pop!™ is a trademark and logo of POP, LLC.

Printed in the United States of America, North Mankato, Minnesota

082018
012019

THIS BOOK CONTAINS RECYCLED MATERIALS

Cover Photo: Sander Meertins/Alamy
Interior Photos: Sander Meertins/Alamy, 1; Gerard Lacz/Science Source, 5 (top); Shutterstock Images, 5 (bottom left), 6, 15, 16; Remo Savisaar/Alamy, 5 (bottom right); Ger Bosma/Alamy, 9; Tom Uhlman/Alamy, 10, 20; E. R. Degginger/Science Source, 13; Bill Curtsinger/National Geographic, 19

Editor: Charly Haley
Series Designer: Laura Mitchell

Library of Congress Control Number: 2018950117
Publisher's Cataloging-in-Publication Data
Names: Gaertner, Meg, author.
Title: Muskrats / by Meg Gaertner.
Description: Minneapolis, Minnesota : Pop!, 2019 | Series: Pond animals | Includes online resources and index.
Identifiers: ISBN 9781532162091 (lib. bdg.) | ISBN 9781641855808 (pbk) | ISBN 9781532163159 (ebook)
Subjects: LCSH: Muskrat--Juvenile literature. | Rodents--Juvenile literature. | Pond animals--Juvenile literature.
Classification: DDC 599.323--dc23

Hello! My name is
Cody Koala

Pop open this book and you'll find QR codes like this one, loaded with information, so you can learn even more!

Scan this code* and others like it while you read, or visit the website below to make this book pop.

popbooksonline.com/muskrats

*Scanning QR codes requires a web-enabled smart device with a QR code reader app and a camera.

Table of Contents

Chapter 1
Water Rodent 4

Chapter 2
Habitat 8

Chapter 3
Food and Predators . . . 14

Chapter 4
Life of a Muskrat 18

Making Connections 22
Glossary. 23
Index 24
Online Resources 24

Chapter 1

Water Rodent

Muskrats are large **rodents**. Their fur is red-brown or gray. They have large back feet for swimming. They have small front feet for digging.

Watch a video here!

Muskrats have long tails. A muskrat's tail is about the same length as the rest of its body. The muskrat uses its tail to **steer** in the water while swimming.

Chapter 2

Habitat

Muskrats live in **marshes**, ponds, and other **habitats** with lots of water plants. They spend time on land and in water.

Learn more here!

Muskrats build homes in or near water. They build **lodges** out of mud and plants.

> Animals such as snakes and ducks like to use muskrat lodges for their nests.

Muskrats also dig burrows underground. These homes can include many rooms and tunnels.

> Muskrats leave a smell to keep animals away from their homes.

Chapter 3

Food and Predators

Muskrats mostly eat plants. But sometimes they eat snails, turtles, and small fish. In the winter, when ponds freeze, muskrats dig to get food underneath the ice.

Learn more here!

15

Many animals like to eat muskrats. These **predators** include otters, eagles, and foxes. Muskrats will fight other animals to stay safe.

Chapter 4

Life of a Muskrat

Mother muskrats give birth to two or three **litters** each summer. There can be up to ten babies in each litter.

Complete an activity here!

Muskrat babies are called kits. They grow fast. Kits can live on their own after four to six weeks.

> Muskrats live about one year in the wild.

Making Connections

Text-to-Self

Have you ever seen a muskrat? If not, have you seen any other animals in the wild?

Text-to-Text

Have you read another book about a different animal? How is that animal similar to a muskrat? How is it different?

Text-to-World

Muskrats build lodges or burrows. What kinds of homes do other animals have?

Glossary

habitat – a place for a plant or animal to live.

litter – a group of young animals born to an adult animal at one time.

lodge – an animal home made of mud and plants.

marsh – wet land usually filled with grass or other plants, also called a swamp.

predator – an animal that hunts and eats other animals.

rodent – a type of animal that has a single pair of strong teeth.

steer – to control movement.

Index

burrows, 12

lodges, 11

marshes, 8

plants, 8–11, 14

ponds, 8, 14

predators, 17

rodents, 4

swimming, 4–7

Online Resources
popbooksonline.com

Thanks for reading this Cody Koala book!

Scan this code* and others like it in this book, or visit the website below to make this book pop!

popbooksonline.com/muskrats

*Scanning QR codes requires a web-enabled smart device with a QR code reader app and a camera.